Designed For Success

Off-Road Vehicles

Revised & Updated

Ian Graham

Heinemann Library
Chicago, Illinois

© 2008 Heinemann Library
a division of Reed Elsevier Inc.
Chicago, Illinois

Customer Service 888-363-4266
Visit our website at www.heinemannraintree.com

Editorial: Andrew Farrow, Patrick Catel, and Harriet Milles
Design: Steven Mead and Geoff Ward
Illustrations: Geoff Ward
Picture Research: Melissa Allison
Production: Alison Parsons

Originated by Modern Age
Printed and bound in China by South China Printing Company

13 12 11 10 09 08
10 9 8 7 6 5 4 3 2 1

Library of Congress Cataloging-in-Publication Data
Graham, Ian, 1953–
  Off-road vehicles / Ian Graham
    p. cm. – (Desgned for success)
Summary: Describes cars, trucks, and other vehicles that are designed to be driven on all sorts of surfaces from dirt to mud or snow and ice.
Includes bibliographical references and index.
  ISBN 978-1-432-91646-6 (Library Binding-hardcover)
1. Off-road vehicles—Juvenile literature. [1. Off-road vehicles. 2. Four-wheel drive vehicles.]
    I. Title. II. Series.
    TL235.6. G72 2003
    629.22'042–dc21

                            2002006118

Acknowledgments
The publishers would like to thank the following for permission to reproduce photographs: © Alvey & Towers pp. **10**, **11** (top), **11** (middle), **11** (bottom), **25** (bottom); © Auto Express pp. **4**, **7** (top), **9** (middle), **12**, **16**, **17**, **18** (left), **24** (bottom), contents; © British Motor Industry Heritage Trust pp. **7** (bottom), **29**; © Camera Press/Susan Goldman p. **6** (bottom); © Corbis pp. **3**, **14**, **15**, **22**; © Corbis/Reuters/Wolfgang Rattay p. **25** (top); © Dutton Maritime Ltd pp. **21** (middle), **21** (bottom); © European Press Agency/PA Photos p. **6** (top); © Holden p. **5** (top); © Jeep World p. **20**; © Land Rover Press Office pp. **5** (bottom), **9** (bottom); © MPL p. **23** (bottom); © National Motor Museum p. **23** (top); © Nick Dimbleby pp. **1**, **9** (top), **12**, **18** (right); © NMM/Dunlop p. **24** (top); © Octagon p. **26**; © PA Photos/Barry Batchelor p. **21** (top); © Ragnar Roberts p. **27** (top); © Superstock p. **28**; © Tografox/R.D. Battersby pp. **13**, **27** (bottom).

Cover photograph reproduced with permission of © Superstock/age fotostock. Background images by © istockphoto/Jan Rihak and © Corbis.

Our thanks to Geoff Teare for his help in the preparation of the first edition of this book.

▷ Contents

Any words appearing in the text in bold, **like this**, are explained in the glossary.

Off-Road Vehicles

What are off-road vehicles (ORVs)? They are cars and trucks that are designed to be driven on all sorts of surfaces. Some ORVs are also known as SUVs (Sport Utility Vehicles). Most cars are designed for use on smooth, hard roads—but if you take them off the road onto a soft, soggy field or dry desert sand, they will quickly sink into the ground or grind to a halt. The wheels will spin fast, but the vehicles will not move because the wheels cannot grip the soft, loose surface. In many countries, there are few paved roads. Many of the roads are dirt tracks that turn to mud when it rains. Rugged vehicles are essential for driving in these conditions.

ORVs must be able to cope with both normal roads and also difficult off-road conditions that defeat other vehicles. An ORV designer has to create a vehicle that can be driven on soft, uneven, loose, or slippery surfaces without stopping, sinking, or skidding. The distinctive shape of an ORV is the result of finding the answers to these design problems.

Classic cruiser ▽

The Toyota Land Cruiser is a classic off-roader. It combines the ability to go almost anywhere, on or off the road, with a very comfortable interior. The **prototype** of the first Land Cruiser was designed in 1950. Since then, its design has been updated year after year. In 1996 and 1998, Land Cruisers took first and second places in the Paris–Dakar rally, a tough motorsport event that crosses part of the Sahara Desert.

TOYOTA LAND CRUISER 3-DOOR

Engine: 3.0-liter **diesel**

Engine power: 170 **hp**

Length: 14.4 feet (4.4 m)

Weight: 4,453 lbs (2,020 kg)

Top speed: 109 mph (175 kph)

Jackaroo ▷

Sometimes the same vehicle is made in different countries under different names. A manufacturer in one country may build its own vehicle using a successful **chassis** (frame) and engine designed by another manufacturer in another country. A "jackaroo" is the name given to a trainee on an Australian sheep or cattle station. It is also an off-road vehicle produced by the Australian carmaker Holden until 2003. Under its Holden bodywork, the Jackaroo was based on the successful Japanese Isuzu Trooper.

All-around rover ▽

Land Rover's Range Rover was introduced in 1970. It made ORVs fashionable. In addition to performing well off-road, it could carry heavy loads and was comfortable enough to be used as a family car. It made many people who never drove off-road want to own an ORV.

The Range Rover is designed to be equally at home on-road or off-road.

Rugged Design

An off-road vehicle designer starts with a list of the challenges the vehicle has to deal with. The designer then figures out a solution for each problem.

When a normal car crosses rough ground, it risks crashing down onto a rock and smashing itself. The first thing a designer does is to raise the vehicle higher so that there is more **ground clearance**. The bottom of the vehicle may also be protected by a thick metal plate. To give the maximum grip, all four wheels are driven by the engine, instead of just two. To give even more grip on soft or loose surfaces, the tires are more deeply grooved than normal car tires. An ORV's rugged construction enables it to keep going on uneven, rocky, or slippery ground without bending or breaking.

The Hummer ▷

The High-Mobility Multipurpose Wheeled Vehicle (HMMWV) is perhaps the ultimate off-road vehicle. It is known as a "Humvee" or "Hummer." It was designed as a **military** replacement for the Jeep, so it can cope with the toughest conditions. The driver can let the tires down or **inflate** them at the press of a switch while the vehicle is still moving. Letting out some air makes the tires crush down and spread out so that they grip soft ground better.

◁ Civilian Hummer

The **civilian** version of the Hummer is about 1.5 feet (0.5 meters) wider than most other off-roaders. Its extra width makes it more difficult to tip over. It can climb steeper slopes than other mass-produced ORVs.

◁ On the farm

Tractors are designed specifically for working off-road. They have to cope with all sorts of surfaces, often while pulling a heavy trailer or machine. Their big wheels give a smoother ride over rough ground or plowed fields. The special tires have thick rubber bars sticking out. They are designed like this so that the bars dig into soft ground and stop the wheels from spinning or sinking.

GENERAL MOTORS "HUMMER" H2

Engine: 6.0-liter V8

Engine power: 329 **hp**

Length: 17.1 feet (5.2 m)

Weight: 6,400 lbs (2,903 kg)

Top speed: 99 mph (160 kph)

Out of trouble ▽

Working ORVs like this early Land Rover are often equipped with a **winch**. An off-roader with a winch can pull itself out of trouble. The cable is pulled out and anchored to a tree. Then the winch can wind the cable in and drag the vehicle out of difficulty.

Extreme Performance

The secret behind an ORV's **performance**, especially in the most extreme conditions, is the way its engine drives the wheels.

It may seem surprising, but a car's wheels often spin at different speeds! When a car turns, the wheels on the outside of the bend travel farther than the wheels on the inside. And the front wheels (used to steer) travel farther than the rear wheels. The car has a device called a **differential**. The differential lets a wheel on one side spin faster than a wheel on the other side. It works well for a family car, but is disastrous for an ORV. If one wheel grips the ground, but the wheel on the other side slips, the differential lets all the engine power go to the slipping wheel. One wheel stops while the other spins wildly. So, ORV designers have found a way of letting the wheels spin at different speeds on normal roads, but locking them together on soft ground.

Different paths ▽

When a normal car turns a corner, its wheels follow slightly different paths along the road. A set of **gears** called a differential is fitted between the two wheels that are driven by the engine. The differential gives out the engine power to the wheels according to how much they need, so that they can turn at different speeds if they need to.

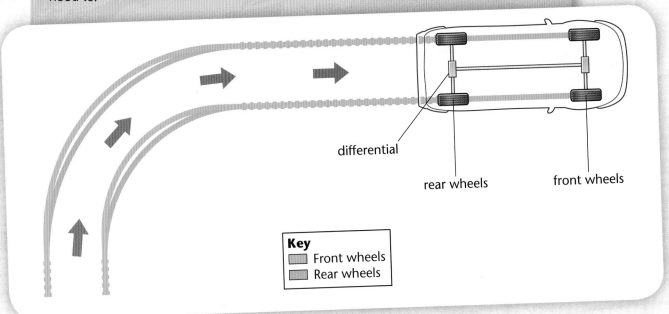

differential

rear wheels

front wheels

Key	
	Front wheels
	Rear wheels

A slippery problem △

The type of differential used in family cars does not work well for off-road driving. When one wheel of an ORV slips and spins on slippery ground, a normal differential would send all the engine power to that wheel and none to the wheel that is gripping the ground. This means the vehicle would stop dead! One answer is to redesign the differential so that the wheels are allowed to have only a small difference in speed between them. This is known as a "limited slip differential." If one wheel loses grip, this system stops it from spinning wildly. Meanwhile the gripping wheel drives the ORV out of trouble.

Sharing power ▽

All four of an ORV's wheels can be driven by the engine, instead of just two. This is called **four-wheel drive (4x4)**. There is one differential between the front wheels and another differential between the rear wheels.

- The front and rear wheels can be linked so that half of the engine power goes to the front wheels and half to the rear wheels.

- Otherwise, they can be linked by a differential so that each of the four wheels receives as much engine power as it needs.

The Range Rover was the first 4x4 with electronic traction control. It automatically applied the brakes to any of the wheels that slipped.

▷ All-Terrain Vehicles

Off-road vehicles come in a range of shapes and sizes. The smallest are **four-wheel drive**, sit-on motors called **all-terrain vehicles (ATVs)**.

ATVs are designed to be go-anywhere off-roaders for one person. They are used for fun, sports, and work, and they are easier to ride than a motorcycle. The rider sits on top and steers by turning the handlebars. Speed is controlled with either a thumb-activated lever on the handlebars or a **twist-grip**, alongside a foot-operated **gearshift**. They have to have good **suspension** to let the wheels follow all the bumps and holes in the ground without bouncing the rider off. ATVs are very stable little vehicles, because the rider sits in the middle of the four wheels. Their built-in stability means that the rider does not have to balance as the vehicle drives over rough ground.

◁ Working ATVs

The Honda FourTrax Foreman 4X4 is a typical modern ATV. It is designed to be a hardworking vehicle. Racks on the front and behind the rider can carry cargo. Bigger loads can be hauled in a trailer. ATVs like this are called utility vehicles. There are also sport models, designed for speed and **performance** instead of rugged pulling power.

FOURTRAX FOREMAN 4X4

Engine: 475 cc

Length: 6.9 feet (2.1 m)

Weight: 595 lbs (270 kg)

Kids' ATVs ▷

ATVs are so easy to ride that some models are designed specially for people under 16. They have smaller engines to make them lighter and easier to handle. A youth ATV might have a 90-**cc** engine, compared to a full-size ATV for an adult rider with an engine of 230 cc to 500 cc. A smaller youth model might weigh just over 220 pounds, about half the weight of a full-size model.

An ATV's design, like this child's version, makes it as easy to service and repair as a motorcycle.

Round 'em up! ▽

An ATV's small size, rugged design, and ease of use make it ideal for farmers to get around their fields and visit their animals. They are used to take food to animals in winter, to round up sheep for shearing, and to carry tools and materials around farms and forests. Many of these jobs used to be done on horseback or by means of larger ORVs. Now, they can be done faster, more easily, and less expensively by ATVs.

Jeep Wrangler
DESIGNING THE BEST

The Jeep Wrangler is designed to cope easily with all conditions, from swamp to sand and everything in between. Its high **ground clearance** of 8.7 inches lets it cross stony land or ground with deep tracks without getting caught up on rocks. It can climb steeply, and its **suspension** lets the wheels travel up and down so far that it can drive over boulders or fallen trees that would trap most other vehicles, even other off-roaders. Its interior is designed to be equally practical. The mats can be taken out, the seats are covered with water-resistant material, and there are drain holes in the floor so that mud and dirt can be washed out. The backseat folds down to create enough storage space for camping equipment or fishing gear.

Without power steering, it would be very difficult to handle the Wrangler in tough conditions like this.

Power steering

It takes a lot of muscle power to turn an ORV's wheels, especially on soft ground. To make it easier, off-roaders like the Wrangler often have power-assisted steering. When the driver turns the steering wheel, a pump forces oil through a pipe—this oil pressure then turns the wheels. The pump and oil magnify the driver's muscle-power and make it easier to steer the vehicle.

JEEP WRANGLER

Engine: 3.8-liter V-6

Engine power: 202 **hp**

Length: 13.5 feet (4.1 m)

Weight: 3,780 lbs (1,715 kg)

Top speed: 112 mph (180 kph)

Springs and things

An ORV designer can choose from two different types of suspension, the springy connection between the vehicle and its wheels.

- Independent suspension lets the wheels move up and down separately. Racing cars use independent suspension. However, loading a vehicle with extra weight makes its **axles** settle lower, making it more likely to hit rocks.

- A different type of suspension, called live axle suspension, keeps the axles and **differentials** at the same height above the ground, no matter how heavily the vehicle is loaded. Working vehicles like the Wrangler use live axle suspension.

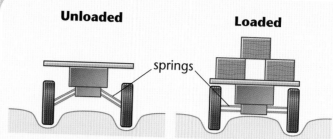

Unloaded **Loaded**

springs

Independent suspension

When the vehicle is loaded up (right), the springs are pressed down and the vehicle settles lower, closer to the ground.

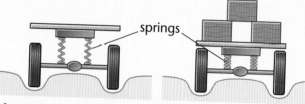

springs

Live axle suspension

The axle is fixed to the **chassis**. The springs fit between the car's body and the chassis. So, when the vehicle is loaded up, compressing the springs, the axle stays at the same height above the ground—this is good for off-road vehicles.

Leaves and coils

Designers are always on the lookout for better ways of building vehicles.

- The first Jeeps had a suspension system made from leaf **springs**. A leaf spring is made from a pile of thin metal strips bent into a curved shape. It is simple and it works, but there are other types of spring that are even better.

- In 1997 the Wrangler's leaf springs were replaced by coil springs, seen in the middle of this photo. Coil springs let the wheels move a greater distance up and down, which makes the new Wrangler more comfortable to travel in.

CLOSER LOOK

Jeep Wrangler

BUILT FOR HARD KNOCKS

Mass-produced ORVs like the Jeep Wrangler are built on an **assembly line**. Assembly begins with the vehicle's chassis. The Wrangler's chassis is a strong metal frame shaped like a ladder. As the chassis moves along the assembly line, the body, engine, suspension, seats, wheels, and all the other parts are added to it until a complete Wrangler is driven off the end of the line.

This sounds simple, but the assembly line has to be designed as carefully as the vehicles that are built on it. It has to move the vehicles along at precisely the right speed. There has to be enough space around it to store the parts needed for each stage of construction. There have to be powered **hoists** to hold and move heavy parts, such as engines. It needs to be well lit and a safe place to work.

Pressing metal

The large metal panels that make the body of the Wrangler are shaped by a method called pressing. To make a door panel, for example, a flat sheet of metal is placed between two metal blocks shaped like the finished panel. On one block, called the punch, the shape of the panel stands out from the surface of the block. The other block, called the die, is hollowed out in the same shape. The punch presses the metal sheet into the hollowed-out die. (Imagine pushing a fist into a cupped hand with a sheet of paper in between them.) The thin metal sheet bends into the shape of the panel.

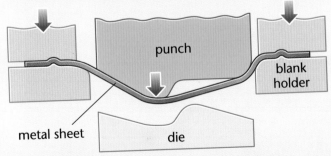

punch

blank holder

metal sheet

die

A blank sheet of metal, which is flat, is pressed into the shape of panel needed.

Booting up

An off-roader's tires are made from a mixture of materials designed to hold air inside, support the vehicle's weight, and transfer its engine power to the ground.

- Rubber is used because it is flexible, airtight, and grips the road.
- Steel hoops embedded in the rubber hold the tire firmly on the wheel rim.
- Strips of tough material (called body plies) laid from side to side give the tire its strength.
- Grooves are molded into the flattened rubber edge of the tire, called the tread. In wet conditions, the tread helps to squeeze water out from under the tire.

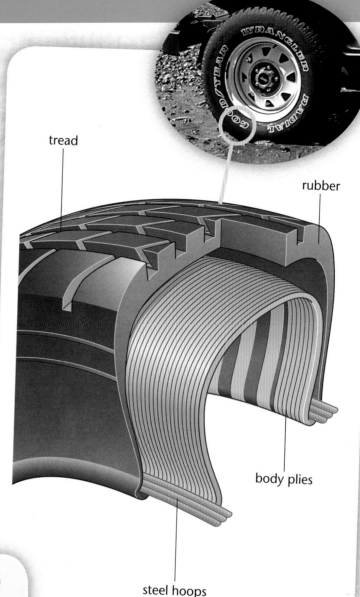

tread

rubber

body plies

steel hoops

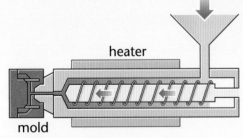

Melted plastic is forced into the mold.

plastic powder/granules in

heater

mold

heater

mold

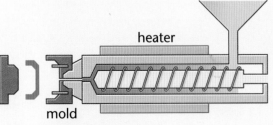

When the plastic has cooled, the mold is opened and the part is removed.

Giving injections

Many of a vehicle's plastic parts are made by a method called "injection molding." It works by heating plastic powder or granules until they melt. The liquid plastic is then forced into a mold. The plastic fills the mold and takes on its shape. When the plastic cools, it changes from liquid to solid. Finally, the mold is opened and the part is taken out.

CLOSER LOOK

Jeep Wrangler
HARD DRIVING

The Wrangler, and every other Jeep, is designed to be able to drive the Rubicon Trail. This winding, rocky trail is famous among off-road drivers. It is the ultimate test of an off-road vehicle's **performance**. It stretches from Loon Lake to Lake Tahoe in northern California and takes two or three days to complete. Parts of it are covered with boulders the size of houses!

The Wrangler's small size and its ability to turn tightly let it get around big boulders. These same features make it just as easy to maneuver in city traffic and park in small spaces. The Wrangler's 3.8-liter engine is designed to supply plenty of power for off-road work. On-road it can **accelerate** from 0 to 60 mph (100 kph) in only 9.4 seconds and reach a top speed of 112 mph (180 kph)—which is faster than many family cars.

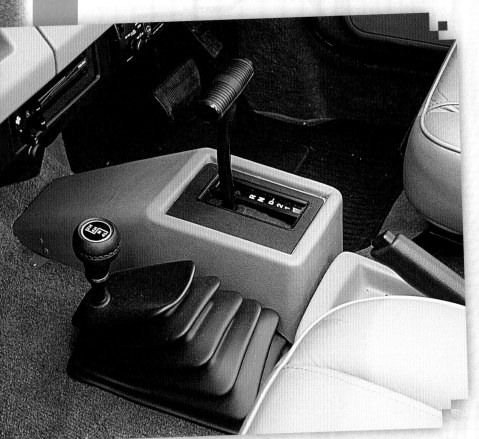

Two wheels or four?

Four-wheel drive is a must for off-road driving, but it is not necessary for driving on roads. The Jeep Wrangler has part-time four-wheel drive. This means the driver can choose whether to use two-wheel or four-wheel drive. Moreover, the driver can switch between the two while the vehicle is moving. This is called changing "on the fly."

The Wrangler looks as if it has two **gear**-changing levers. The lever on the right is a gear lever. The lever on the left is actually used to switch between two-wheel drive and four-wheel drive.

Torque talk

The Wrangler has a 202-horsepower engine, but for off-road vehicle designers, a second figure is just as important. It is called "torque." A vehicle will not move unless its engine applies a force to turn the wheels. This turning force is called torque. An ORV standing in mud needs more torque to start its wheels moving than a car sitting on a flat, hard road. In fact, the Wrangler's engine produces as much torque as some high-performance sports cars.

Computerized brakes

Like many vehicles, the Jeep Wrangler is fitted with a computerized system called ABS (anti-lock braking system). This lets it stop without skidding, no matter how hard the driver presses the brake pedal. ABS senses the speed of each wheel. If a wheel locks (stops turning) and starts to skid, the brakes are automatically released and then re-applied. The vehicle comes to a halt steadily, without skidding. ORVs also use ABS to stop the wheels from spinning when they lose grip on a slippery surface.

On a normal road surface

Off-road vehicle wheel sitting on hard ground

small torque needed to start the wheel moving

wheel turns easily on a hard surface

Off-road

Off-road vehicle wheel in soft mud

more torque needed to overcome the mud's resistance and start the wheel turning

mud makes the wheel more difficult to turn

ABS can stop wheels from spinning in very wet conditions.

A sensor in each wheel sends electronic signals along wires (red) to a control box. If a wheel spins too fast, the control box operates the brake on that wheel to slow it down.

ABS control box

CLOSER LOOK

Engine Power

Off-road vehicles are powered by a variety of different engines, from tiny **two-strokes** to massive **diesels**. The designer chooses the engine to suit the size and weight of the vehicle and what it will be used for.

Two-stroke engines power the smallest **ATVs** and snowmobiles. They are small, simple engines, but they wear out faster than other engines and they produce more air pollution. Larger vehicles are powered by **four-stroke engines**. There are two types, designed to burn different fuels. The simplest and most rugged is the diesel engine. The rest are powered by gasoline engines. Whatever the engine type, they all work by burning fuel to push a **piston** down inside a **cylinder**. The up-and-down motion of the piston, or pistons, turns the vehicle's wheels.

A four-stroke gasoline engine needs a battery to make the electric sparks that **ignite** the fuel and a radiator to cool the water that flows around the engine.

battery

radiator

ORVs have enormous engine power, not only for driving in difficult conditions, but also for operating equipment, such as **winches**. A winch can be used to pull a vehicle out of trouble if it gets stuck in particularly heavy mud.

Four-stroke

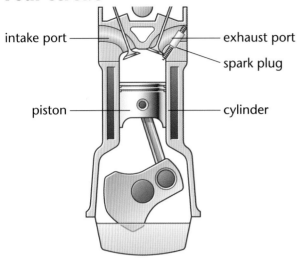

intake port
exhaust port
spark plug
piston
cylinder

Two-stroke

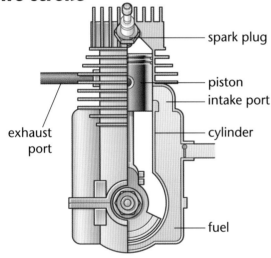

spark plug
piston
intake port
cylinder
exhaust port
fuel

Diesel

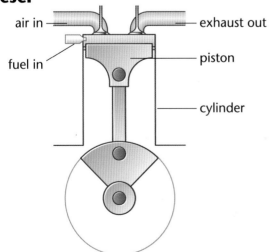

air in
exhaust out
fuel in
piston
cylinder

◁ Four-stroke

Many ORVs are powered by four-stroke gasoline engines. Each of the four "strokes" is an up or down movement of one of the engine's pistons inside a cylinder. As the piston moves down the cylinder, it sucks air in through the intake port. Fuel is sprayed into the air. The piston moves up and crushes the air. An electric spark from the spark plug ignites the fuel. The burning fuel heats the air, which pushes the piston down the cylinder. As it rises again, it pushes the burned gases out through the **exhaust** port.

◁ Two-stroke

When a spark ignites the fuel in a two-stroke engine, the piston is forced down the cylinder. On its way, it uncovers a pipe called the exhaust port and the hot gases rush out through it. The piston continues moving down until it uncovers a second pipe called the intake port. A fresh supply of fuel and air rush into the cylinder, the piston rises, and the cycle begins all over again.

◁ Diesel

A diesel engine does not use an electric spark to ignite its fuel. When a piston crushes the air inside a cylinder, the air gets hotter and hotter. As soon as the fuel is sprayed into the cylinder, the air is so hot that the fuel ignites by itself. The air is crushed so much that the engine has to be made very strong to stop it from bursting apart. Because of this, diesel engines are bigger and heavier than gasoline engines.

Amphibious Cars

Off-road vehicles can drive easily through a few inches of water, but an **amphibious** vehicle can be driven straight into the deepest river, lake, or even the sea, because it floats.

Amphibious vehicles work like normal cars on a road and like motorboats in water. To make a car behave like a motorboat, it has to be designed like a motorboat. A motorboat needs a watertight **hull** to stop water from leaking inside, so an amphibious car needs a watertight body, too. A motorboat needs a way of propelling itself through the water, and so does an amphibious vehicle. The simplest way to move an amphibious car through water is to let its wheels do the work. Off-road tires spinning underwater can move a floating car along at walking pace. To go faster, or to cope with stronger water currents, the car needs a **propeller** to push it through the water.

Jeep-boat ▽

Most of the hundred or so different amphibious vehicles built so far have been **military**. One of the first was based on the famous World War II (1939–45) Jeep. It was called the Ford GPA "Seep." In water it was powered by a propeller driven by the Jeep's engine. The Seep was intended to ferry troops from ships to the shore. About 5,000 of them were built.

◁ The one and only Amphicar

The only **civilian** amphibious car that ever went into mass production was the Amphicar. About 3,500 of them were produced in the 1960s. It used parts from several other cars—including Mercedes brakes and **suspension**, Porsche **transmission**, and a Triumph Herald engine. Its body was made from steel. In the water, it was powered by propellers driven by the engine. It was steered simply by turning the front wheels.

Mariner ▷

The Dutton Commander is a modern amphibious car. The body is made from **GRP (glass reinforced plastic)**, because, unlike steel, GRP does not rust. In water, it is powered by a **water-jet** from a 8-inch (20-centimeter) propeller. In 2006 two Dutton amphibious cars crossed the English Channel in just over seven hours.

DUTTON COMMANDER AMPHIBIOUS CAR

Engine: 1.3 liters

Engine power: 85 **hp**

Length: 15.4 feet (4.7 m)

Weight: 2,535 lbs (1,150 kg)

Speed in water: 6 mph (10 kph)

Dune Buggies

Most off-road vehicles are designed to do a job, but dune buggies are recreational vehicles—they are for having fun. These skeleton-like cars are designed for thrilling, fast drives on sand.

A dune buggy begins as a frame made from steel tubes welded together. The engine is usually placed at the back, where its weight helps press the big rear tires down into the sand to get more grip. A Volkswagen 1,600-**cc** or 2-liter engine is a popular choice. Most dune buggies are two-seaters, but by lengthening the frame, two more passenger seats can be fit in. The majority of dune buggies are one-offs built by their owners. But they are now so popular, especially in the United States, that manufacturers have started to produce kits of parts and even complete cars.

Leaping off sand dunes is all part of the fun of driving a dune buggy.

Safety first ▽

The most important part of a dune buggy is its roll bar or roll cage—a high bar or metal frame that loops over above the driver's head. If the buggy gets flipped over and lands upside down, the roll bar or cage is designed to support the car's weight and stop the people inside from being crushed.

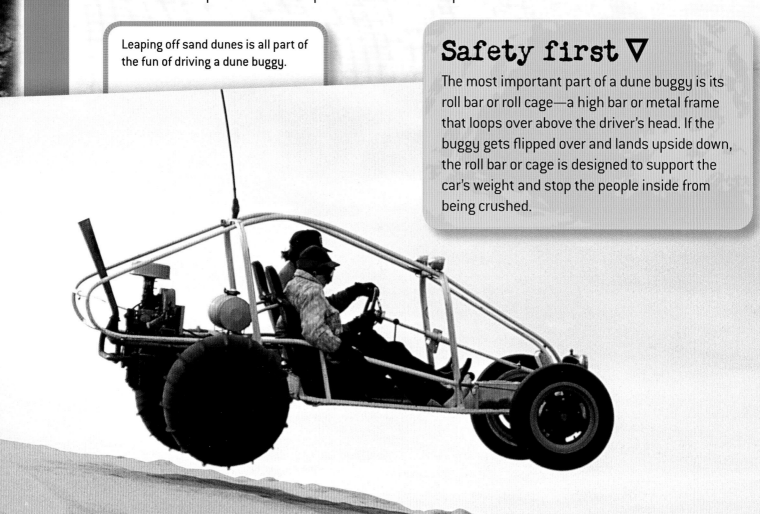

◁ Sand blasters

People started having off-road fun with the Beach Buggy in the early 1960s. The dune buggies being built at that time were heavy and cumbersome. Then boat designer Bruce Meyers used his knowledge of building lightweight **fiberglass** boats to redesign the dune buggy. He put a fiberglass body on a shortened, rear-engined Volkswagen **chassis**. The result was an off-roader that was light, fast, and a lot of fun. Thousands of Beach Buggies were sold in kit form for people to build themselves.

Military buggies ▽

Special forces often operate in small groups traveling fast and light. They race ahead of troops to scout out the land ahead, spy on enemy forces, and strike wherever they can. Normal **military** ORVs are too big for their needs. Dune buggies are perfect. Military dune buggies, or "fast attack vehicles," must be reliable, because a breakdown could leave troops stranded in enemy territory. For use in the desert, a good air filter is also essential. It stops sand from being sucked into the engine and damaging it.

▷ Snow Vehicles

In some countries, the roads become covered in snow and ice every year, so even "on-road vehicles" have to cope with off-road conditions.

Snow and ice are especially difficult to drive on, even in an off-road vehicle, because they are so slippery. A vehicle has to be able to grip the surface in order to **accelerate**, brake, and steer. Without grip, it cannot do any of these things. One answer is to fit a standard ORV with tires designed to bite into slippery ground. Extra-chunky winter tires can deal with snow and ice on normal roads, but thick ice needs a different design solution—studded tires. They are covered with hundreds of steel studs or spikes that bite into the ice.

Really deep snow is too much for any normal off-roader, even one fitted with studded tires. These extreme conditions need a whole new vehicle specially designed for the purpose. The answer is the snowmobile!

Studs: Good or bad? ▷

Studded tires give ORVs grip on ice, but they can damage roads. In Norway, about 275,000 tons of **asphalt** is worn off the roads every year by studded tires. Repairing this damage is very expensive. It is also bad for the environment and perhaps for people, too. Some of the dust produced by stud damage is blown up into the air, adding to air pollution, and some of it is breathed in by people.

Four-wheel drive is essential for driving on snow and ice, because all four wheels grip the slippery surface. A family car is more likely to slip and slide because only two wheels grip the ground.

◁ Off-road at the poles

Snowmobiles are great for carrying one or two people and pulling light loads. A bigger and more powerful vehicle is needed to haul heavy loads. In the polar regions, large-tracked snowcats carry people and goods. The broad tracks spread the vehicle's weight and stop it from sinking. They drive the vehicle and also steer it. When the track on one side is stopped, the other track pushes the vehicle around into a turn.

YAMAHA APEX RTX SNOWMOBILE

Engine: 998 **cc**, 4-**cylinder**	
Engine power: 150 **hp**	
Length: 9.2 feet (2.8 m)	
Weight: 550 lbs (250 kg)	

Snowmobiles ▽

In parts of North America, Scandinavia, Russia, and the polar regions, the ground is permanently covered with snow. ORVs can cope with thin or hard-packed snow, but a different type of vehicle is needed to go into the deep, off-road snow. Snowmobiles are small one- or two-person snow-bikes with skis and a **continuous track** instead of wheels. The engine drives the track. Steering is by means of turning the ski, or skis, at the front.

▷ Off-Road Sports

Almost all types of motor vehicle, from lawn mowers to trucks, take part in motor racing. Off-road vehicles are raced against each other, too. They compete in some of the most extreme motorsport events in the world.

There are two main types of off-road racing that use two very different types of vehicle. Vehicles that look like ordinary production ORVs take part in races and rallies across deserts in the United States, Australia, Africa, the Middle East, and Asia. Some of them are ordinary ORVs. Others are production models that have been specially prepared for racing. Formula Offroad racing is completely different. Its vehicles start out as standard off-roaders, but they are completely rebuilt, often with parts from other vehicles. They look like a collection of scrapyard leftovers bolted together, but they are extremely powerful and strong machines.

On safari ▽

The Australian Safari is one of the toughest tests of off-road vehicles and their drivers and is over 33,100 miles (5,000 kilometers) long. The vehicles are modified as much as the regulations allow.

- Some of them are almost standard ORVs straight out of the showroom, with a few minor modifications for safety and long-range driving.
- Others are specially built for racing, with tougher **suspension**, a stronger under-body, and a race-tuned engine.

Arctic racers ▷

Formula Offroad is one of the most exciting forms of off-road racing. It began in Iceland in the 1980s. There is now also a Nordic Formula Offroad championship, which has races in Sweden, Norway, Denmark, and Finland. The strange-looking vehicles can climb almost vertical slopes. They are based on standard ORVs, but very little of the original vehicle remains.

- The **chassis** and suspension are beefed up to make them as strong as a tank.
- The standard engine is replaced by a much more powerful one.
- The tires have scoops or plates sticking out to grip soft, muddy ground.

Racing classes of Formula Offroad:

- Modified: The racing vehicle must have a body similar to a production vehicle.
- Unlimited: Almost anything is allowed, within certain safety limits.

◁ Strapping in

Off-road racing drivers are thrown in all directions as their vehicles bounce around the roughest courses. To stop them from flying out of the car altogether, they are tightly strapped into their seats by a specially designed racing harness. It takes longer to belt up than a standard car seatbelt because there are more straps to clip in place, but it holds a driver more securely.

Data Files

Some of the most popular off-road vehicles are listed below.

Off-road vehicle	Engine	Power (horsepower)	Length (feet)	Weight (pounds)
Chevrolet Tahoe	5.3-liter V8	320	16.7	5,527
Dutton Commander **Amphibious** car	1.3-liter inline 4	85	15.4	2,535
Ford Explorer	4.0-liter V6	210	16.1	unknown
General Motors Hummer H2	6.0-liter V8	329	17.1	6,400
Honda FourTrax Foreman **ATV**	475 **cc**	unknown	6.9	595
Isuzu Ascender	4.2-liter inline 6	291	16.1	4,592
Jeep Wrangler	3.8-liter V-6	202	13.5	3,780
Land Rover LR2	3.2-liter inline 6	230	14.8	4,254
Mitsubishi New Shogun	3.2-liter inline 4	168	14.4	4,575
Nissan Xterra	4.0-liter V6	261	14.8	4,359
Range Rover	3.6-liter V8	267	16.4	5,990
Subaru Forester	2.5-liter flat 4	230	14.8	3,274
Suzuki Grand Vitara	2.7-liter V6	185	14.8	3,461
Toyota Land Cruiser 3-door	3.0-liter **diesel**	170	14.4	4,453
Yamaha Apex RTX snowmobile	998 cc, 4-**cylinder**	150	9.2	550

The U.S. Army Jeep became the first modern ORV when it was designed in the 1930s. About 700,000 Jeeps were built between 1941 and 1945, for use by the U.S. Army during World War II.

Books

Healy, Nick. *High Mobility Vehicles: The Humvee*. Mankato, Minn.: Edge, 2005.
Maurer, Tracy Nelson. *Hummer (Full Throttle)*. Vero Beach, Fla.: Rourke, 2007.
Maurer, Tracy Nelson. *Jeep (Full Throttle)*. Vero Beach, Fla.: Rourke, 2007.
Mead, Sue. *Off-Road Racing*. New York: Chelsea House, 2005.

Websites

You can find out more about the world's off-road vehicles by looking at the following websites:

http://auto.howstuffworks.com/four-wheel-drive.htm
A website that gives simple explanations of how lots of different things work, including engines, four-wheel drive, and differentials

www.amphicars.com
A website full of information about amphibious cars, mainly the Amphicar

www.jeep.com
The home website of the jeep, including the Jeep Wrangler

http://en.wikipedia.org/wiki/Off-road_vehicle
The history and technology of off-road vehicles

www.hummer.com
The official website of the Hummer vehicle

Few vehicles can compete with the Land Rover's off-road **performance**. The first Land Rover was created in 1948. It was used in farming, forestry, and the construction industry—in fact, anywhere where people needed to drive off-road or carry some equipment with them.

Glossary

accelerate go faster

all-terrain vehicle (ATV) four-wheel, sit-on vehicle

amphibious designed to travel on land and in water

asphalt mixture of bitumen (a black, oily, sticky substance) and gravel, used to surface roads

assembly line series of machines and workers (or robots) that build vehicles, piece by piece, in a factory

axle rod or shaft designed to spin

cc cubic centimeter—a box-shaped volume (space) measuring 1 centimeter (0.4 inch) wide, high, and deep. An engine's size, measured in cubic centimeters, is the size of the space inside its cylinders.

chassis frame on which a vehicle is built

civilian non-military

continuous track endless belt used to spread a vehicle's weight on soft ground or snow so that it does not sink. The belt is driven around by the engine to move the vehicle.

cylinder tube inside an engine where the fuel is burned. The smallest engines have one cylinder. Most off-road vehicles have between four and eight cylinders.

diesel engine type of engine. The main difference between a diesel engine and a gasoline engine is that a diesel engine does not use a spark to ignite the fuel inside the engine. Instead, it crushes the fuel so hard that it heats up until it ignites on its own.

differential set of gears that lets two wheels spin at different speeds

exhaust hot gases that flow out of an engine when fuel is burned

fiberglass material made from mats of hair-thin strands of glass embedded in hard plastic

four-stroke engine type of engine that produces power on every fourth stroke (movement) of each of its pistons

four-wheel drive (4x4) type of vehicle transmission in which all four wheels are driven by the engine. Four-wheel drive gives better grip on soft ground.

gear metal wheel with teeth around the edge. When the teeth of different wheels lock together, an engine turning one wheel makes the other wheel (and anything attached to it) turn, too.

gearshift lever used for changing gear, to go faster or slower

glass reinforced plastic (GRP) material made from thin glass fibers embedded in plastic. A GRP part is made in a mold while the plastic is soft. The plastic then hardens to form a tough, lightweight part.

ground clearance space underneath a vehicle between the ground and the bottom of the vehicle. ORVs have a high ground clearance so that rocks can pass underneath them.

hoist lifting machine

horsepower (hp) unit of measurement of the power of an engine equal to the work done by one horse, or 746 watts of electrical power

hull watertight part of a boat's body that sits in the water

ignite set on fire

inflate enlarge by filling up with gas. A car's tires are inflated with air.

military to do with a country's armed forces

performance way a vehicle functions—its speed, acceleration, stability, and so on

piston drum-shaped part of an engine that slides up and down inside each cylinder. Each piston is pushed down its cylinder by burning fuel in the cylinder. The up-down movements of the pistons turns the vehicle's wheels.

propeller device with blades set at an angle in a central hub. When a boat's propeller spins, the blades push against the water and push, or propel, the boat through the water.

prototype first model of a new vehicle, built for testing

special forces highly trained soldiers who take on the most difficult and dangerous missions, often working in small groups inside enemy territory

spring device, usually made from steel, that bounces back into shape when it is crushed or bent

suspension set of springs and other devices that connect a vehicle's frame to its axles. The suspension system lets the wheels follow bumps and hollows in the ground, while the rest of the vehicle moves along more smoothly.

transmission gears, shafts, and other mechanical parts that transmit an engine's power to its wheels

twist-grip type of hand-grip used by motorcycles and four-wheel ATVs. Twisting the hand-grip makes the engine speed up or slow down.

two-stroke engine type of engine that produces power on every second stroke (movement) of each of its pistons

water-jet type of engine that works by pumping water out as a high-speed jet

winch drum driven by an engine or electric motor. As the drum rotates, it pulls in a cable or rope that is wound around the drum.

Index

OFF-ROAD VEHICLES